# This Book Belogs To

---------------------------------------------------

---------------------------------------------------

---------------------------------------------------

# I SPY with my little eye someting beginning with......

# A Is for

# Air Conditioner

# I SPY with my little eye someting beginning with......

# B Is for

# Beach Ball

# I SPY with my little eye someting beginning with......

**c**

**C** Is for

**Crab**

# I SPY with my little eye someting beginning with......

# I Spy With My Little Eye Someting Beginning With......

# E Is for

# Exercise

# I SPY with my little eye someting beginning with......

**F**

# I SPY with my little eye someting beginning with......

# I SPY with my little eye someting beginning with......

# H Is for

# Hiking

# I SPY with my little eye someting beginning with......

# I Is for

# Ice-cream

# I SPY with my little eye someting beginning with......

# J Is for

# Jet ski

# I SPY with my little eye someting beginning with......

# K Is for

# Kayak

# I SPY with my little eye someting beginning with......

# L Is for

# life jacket

# I SPY with my little eye someting beginning with......

# M Is for

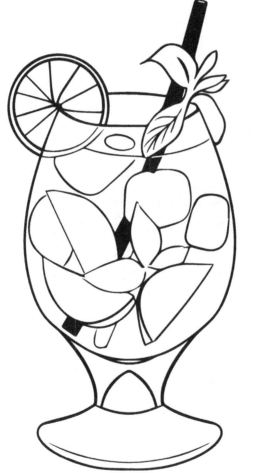

# Mocktail

# I SPY with my little eye someting beginning with......

# I SPY with my little eye someting beginning with......

# I SPY with my little eye someting beginning with......

# P Is for

# Palm Tree

# I SPY with my little eye someting beginning with......

# Q Is for

# Quad Bike

# I SPY with my little eye someting beginning with......

# R Is for

# Relaxation

# I SPY with my little eye someting beginning with......

# S Is for

# Surfing

# I SPY with my little eye someting beginning with......

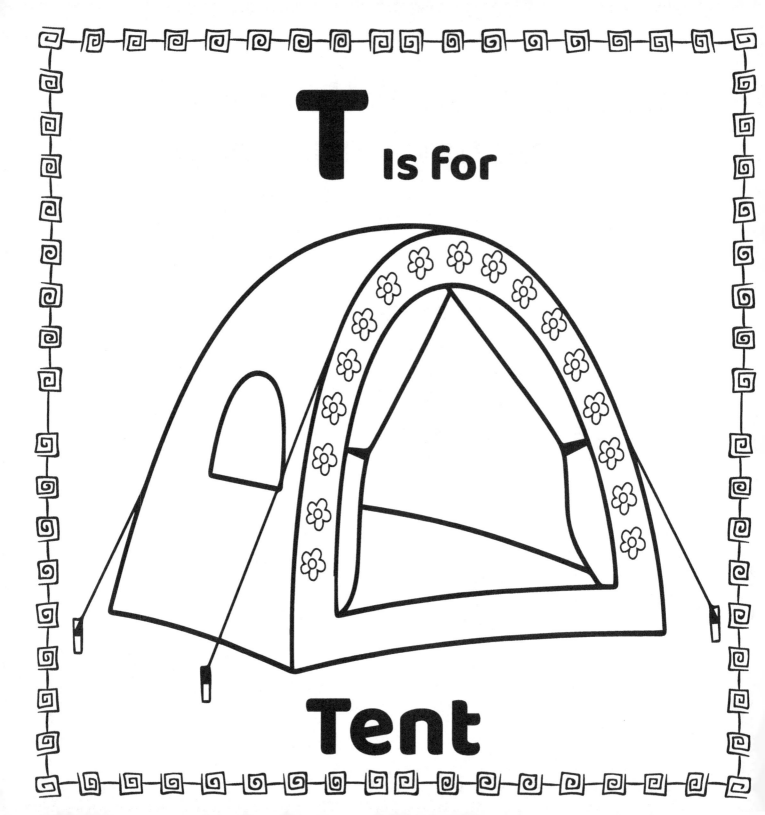

# I SPY with my little eye someting beginning with......

# U Is for

# Umbrella

# I SPY with my little eye someting beginning with......

# V Is for

# Van

# I SPY with my little eye someting beginning with......

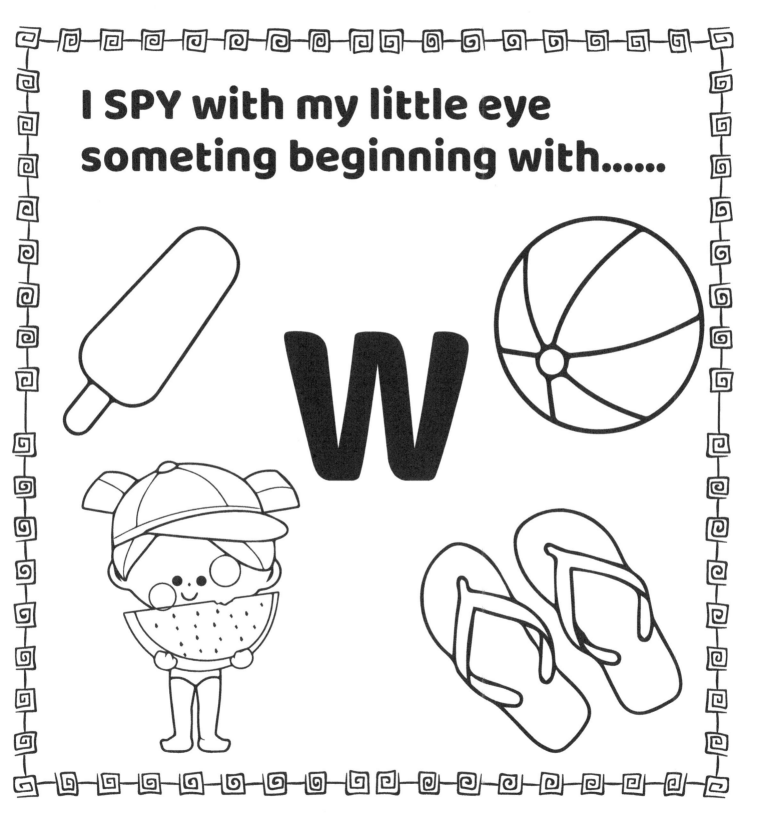

# W Is for

# Watermelon

# I SPY with my little eye someting beginning with......

**X** Is for

**Xebac**

# I SPY with my little eye someting beginning with......

Y Is for

Yacht

# I SPY with my little eye someting beginning with......

# Z Is for

# Zoris

Made in the USA
Monee, IL
13 May 2022

96363449R00031